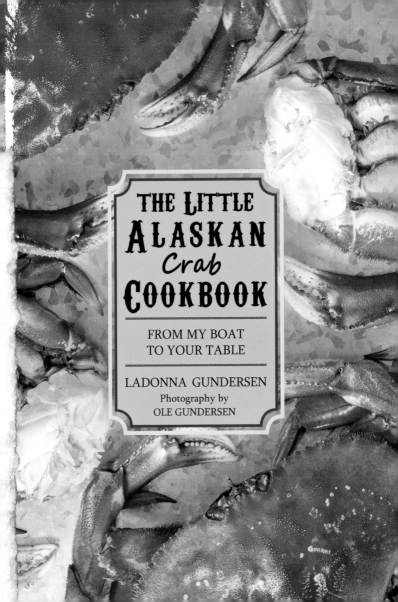

THE LITTLE ALASKAN Crab COOKBOOK

FROM MY BOAT TO YOUR TABLE

LADONNA GUNDERSEN

Photography by
OLE GUNDERSEN

Published
by *LaDonna Rose Publishing*
Book and cover design
by Ole and LaDonna Gundersen
www.ladonnarose.com
www.facebook.com/ladonnarosecooks

Prepress and technical assistance
by Crystal Burrell, Todd Communications

First printing March, 2019
ISBN: 978-1-57833-720-0

Distributed by
Todd Communications
611 E. 12th Ave., Suite 102
Anchorage, Alaska 99501-4603
(907) 274-TODD (8633)
Fax (907) 929-5550
With offices in:
Juneau and Fairbanks, Alaska
sales@toddcom.com
WWW.ALASKABOOKSANDCALENDARS.COM

Printed in China, through **Alaska Print Brokers**,
Anchorage, Alaska.

CONTENTS

LET'S GET STARTED

Here's what we're about; why we wrote this book and the stars of the show

6

SMALL BITES

Tasty starters with the fresh taste of the sea

13

BRUNCH & LUNCH

Bring the ocean to your kitchen with these recipes that are sure to excite your taste buds all day long

27

SOUPS & SALADS

Easy and delicious sums up these quick-to-fix meals

39

MAIN DISHES

You'll get hooked on these recipes inspired at sea

51

SWEET TREATS

These are quick to make and even quicker to eat

75

INDEX

84

Let's Get Started!

Majestic snowy mountains, fast-rushing rivers, pristine icy waters and rugged coastal shores. This is where many Alaskans go to work every day. They also live their lives here, amid the wild unspoiled beauty that is Alaska.

It has been this way for the proud people of Alaska for hundreds, even thousands of years. Families and whole communities depend on it. These are the people who help bring the seafood to your table. Like all entrepreneurs, their success is all about sacrifice and hard work - and hope, sometimes against all odds. Each is a specialist, harvesting a particular variety of fish (salmon, halibut, crab, shrimp) by a specific method that represents the most ecologically sound stainability practices. And each is a jack-of-all-trades: boat mechanic, weather observer, net mender, hands-on-small business owner. But they all believe passionately in the product they sell: some of the finest seafood the world has to offer.

Mystique surrounds seafood cooking. Some of the mystery is appropriate: Here are these shelled creatures of the deep that are delicately flavored and yes a little demanding on the stove or grill or in the oven or pot. But therein lies the attraction. And cooked right, shellfish can become some of the most delightful and rewarding dishes you've ever created. The challenge is approachable, even conquerable. That's what *The Little Alaskan Crab Cookbook* is all about.

Perfectly cooked fresh crab is a true taste sensation. With it's slight firmness and subtle, sweet flavor, crab is nicely accented by a squeeze of lemon, dipped in warmed butter, with a spoonful of cocktail sauce, plenty of napkins and a nice cold beverage. If you want to go beyond that simple yet delicious method, you will enjoy the uncomplicated dishes in this little book.

The crab dishes in this book can be made from any variety of crab, including King, Dungeness, Blue, Rock, Snow and Stone. They all have a similar rich, distinctive, salty-sweet flavor and lend themselves to a variety of delicious, quick to prepare recipes. Most of the dishes can be prepared in 30 minutes tops and most can be easily doubled.

To accomplish this, I focused on everyday ingredients and recipes that would not take too much time and effort—crab dishes you can make anytime, anywhere, quickly and easily. It's fun food, nothing too fancy, but it's all deeply satisfying. As you flip through the recipes, you will find classic favorites like Crab Mac & Cheese, Crab Eggs Benedict and Crab Louie Salad as well as fresh ideas that capture the flavors of cuisines around the world, but have become familiar favorites because of their broad appeal. Some are quick and simple to prepare, others are a more labor of love - but all are delicious additions to a cook's repertoire of recipes. There really is something for everyone to try and enough scope to spoil yourself.

We hope you enjoy the crab dishes you make and the time you spend making it. We hope you will cook often and with family and friends, the way Alaska people do, feeding themselves body and soul.

— Ole & LaDonna

THE STARS OF THE SHOW

KING CRAB

A POPULAR INDULGENCE, REGAL AND DELICIOUS
No other shellfish in the world makes quite the impression of Alaska King Crab. Unmatched for its sweet flavor and rich, yet tender texture, the largest of Alaska's three crab species is a luxury with wide consumer appeal.

REMARKABLY EASY TO SERVE
Cleaned and precooked, Alaska King Crab is simple to prepare. The succulent white body meat and sweet, full, flavorful legs can be served as-is in the shell or used as an indulgent ingredient in recipes.

PRESTIGE AND VERSATILITY
Rich, delicious and luxurious, Alaska King Crab delivers on the '"wow"' factor, whether it's served simply, enhanced by special sauce or used in signature preparations from stir-fried crab legs with garlic butter to an elegant Alaska King Crab Louie salad or Creamy Crabmeat Fettuccine.

SNOW CRAB

FLAVORFUL, ELEGANT, WIDELY APPEALING
Alaska Snow Crab is truly one-of-a-kind shellfish that's simple yet distinctive, with delicately sweet, snowy white flesh that supports its tremendous value and widespread popularity. The trademark big clusters guarantee a memorable presentation, dramatic alone as an appetizer or entrée or as the centerpiece of a salad, soup, surf-and-turf, seafood platter or buffet.

GREAT VALUE AND VERSATILITY

Alaska Snow Crab is recognized as one of today's best shellfish values, thanks to its delicious flavor, stunning appearance and ease of preparation. It also enjoys widespread consumer appeal whether steamed, sautéed or broiled.

DUNGENESS CRAB

THE CONNOISSEUR'S CRAB, DISTINCTIVE AND DELICIOUS

With its one-of-a-kind sweet, almost nutty flavor and tender, flaky white meat, Alaska Dungeness Crab is developing a reputation as the best kept secret in crab; distinctive yet versatile and an exceptional value due to its ease of preparation.

TRADITIONAL YET INNOVATIVE

Traditionally served whole, hot or cold, with melted butter or dipping sauces. Dungeness crab is also surprisingly versatile in salads, sandwiches, appetizers, pastas or specialties such as Dungeness Crab Cakes.

HARVESTED FOR QUALITY AND CONSISTENCY

All Alaska Seafood is wild and pure, responsibly managed for continuing abundance. Alaska crab harvesting seasons are timed to ensure optimum quality and are strictly limited to ensure sustainability. Alaska Dungeness Crab is harvested from the pristine, icy waters of the North Pacific and available frozen for year-round use.

courtesy of alaskaseafood.org

CRABMEAT
Fresh Dungeness Crab is an Alaskan favorite with far reaching appeal. Follow our tips and pick the right kind for your recipe and budget.

LUMP

Also known as "colossal," this grade consists of large pieces of crabmeat and is the most prized. Lump is also the most expensive grade, so don't break it up; splurge on it when a recipe calls for whole large pieces, such as crab cocktails, salads, pasta dishes and casseroles, where you want fork-friendly chunks.

BACKFIN & FLAKE

Backfin grade is made up of smaller, broken chunks of lump crabmeat mixed in with flakes of white body meat. It is less expensive than lump crabmeat but has good flavor and enough texture to look appealing in dishes where the crabmeat is somewhat visible, such as salads, pasta dishes and crab cakes.

CLAW MEAT

Unlike higher grades from the crab's body, claw meat has a strong taste and darker color. This least expensive crabmeat adds pronounced flavor to dips and soups; it's fine in crab cakes but best combined with other grades.

HOW TO PICK THROUGH CRABMEAT

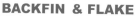

Through the harvesting and packaging process, bits of crab shell and cartilage occasionally slip through and make it into the container. As with all shellfish, biting into a bit of shell or gritty sand can ruin a dish. Avoid this by laying out the crabmeat on a baking sheet. Work in batches keeping the remaining crabmeat refrigerated. Piece by piece, go through the crabmeat and gently squeeze the lumps with your fingertips, discarding any shells or cartilage. Work gently so as not to break up the lumps. Refrigerate the "picked over" portion and repeat the process. 10

Bri Joy Photography

HOW TO CHOOSE AND STORE CRAB

If you want the freshest crab possible - without going fishing - buy it live, take it home and crack it yourself. Here are eight great tips.

1) If you have the good fortune of living in a coastal community, find out where the local fisherman's wharf is and head there for the freshest catch. Whenever possible, buy from local waters when in season.

2) Perkiness is a perk: Peer in the tank and choose one that's quick and alert. Shells should be brightly colored and moist.

3) Heavy is better: If you pick up a large crab that is not heavy, put it back. It won't have as much meat in it as it looks like it would.

4) Look at the legs: Choose a crab that have all their legs, especially if you buy a crab that has already been cooked. Missing legs mean the crab was stressed or over-cooked. The meat will be tough and hard to get out of the shell.

5) How many people per crab? The general rule is two people per Dungeness crab, unless the crab is smaller than 1½ pounds, at which point, play it safe and have one crab per person. For groups larger than four, throw in one extra crab for the pot.

6) If buying frozen crab legs, thaw them overnight in your refrigerator.

7) If you purchase thawed crab legs, use them within a day or two and don't refreeze them - it will damage the sweet, delicate meat.

8) Keep the crab on ice and store it upside-down on it's shell to keep all the juices inside.

ABOUT THE RECIPES

Read each recipe through before you start. There's nothing worse than not having an ingredient or missing a step. It's key to be prepared, so make sure you understand what you have to do in advance.

Draining and Squeezing Crab-meat:
Before you make a recipe, gently squeeze the crabmeat with your hands to remove excess liquid and at the same time feel for any bits of shell and remove them.

Mixing and Handling:
Treat your crab with care. Fold the crabmeat into the recipe as if you are folding cream into a mousse.

Salt:
Some crabmeat is very salty. Taste your crabmeat first and adjust the salt in the recipe accordingly.

The cure for anything
is salt water, sweat,
tears or the sea.
— Isak Dinesen

HOW TO COOK AND CLEAN DUNGENESS CRAB

By following a few simple steps, you can be on your way to serving and enjoying delicious Dungeness Crab.

fig 1
Bring water to a boil.
Bring a large pot of salted water to a rolling boil.

fig 2
Boil the crab.
Carefully drop your crabs into the water and allow it to return to a boil. Once it is boiling again, start your timer. You want to boil the crabs for 10 minutes per pound.

fig 3
Drain crabs. You will be able to tell that your crabs are cooked because their shells should have turned from a blue/grey color to a bright orange hue. Once cooked, pour the pot of water over a colander to drain the crabs.

fig 4
Rinse under cool water.
After your crabs have been drained, run cool water over them. If you are serving them right away, be careful not to make them too cool.

fig 5
Remove the "apron."
Place the crab on a clean work surface, belly side up. Then carefully remove the triangular shaped flap, known as the "apron." Discard this. If there is liquid inside the crab, drain this now.

fig 6
Remove the "carapace." Holding the crab vertically, gently pull the top shell away from the body, using your thumb and fingers, until it comes off. You can wash the top shell and set it aside, in case you want to use it in your presentation.

fig 7
Discard the gills and mouth. With the crab on your work surface belly side down, carefully pull off the spongy gills and mouth on the front of the crab.

Discard those.

fig 8
Rinse the body. After you have discarded all of the unnecessary parts, hold the body under running water to remove any dark matter or debris. Be careful not to remove any of the meat while doing so.

fig 9
Break the crab in half.
With the crab belly side down, grab it on either side using both of your hands. Using a firm motion, push down on both sides and crack the crab in half.

fig 10
Remove the legs.
Insert your thumb and forefinger at each leg joint and twist off each claw and leg. You should remove a bit of the body with each leg. Then using a mallet or small hammer, crack the legs at each joint.

Enjoy!

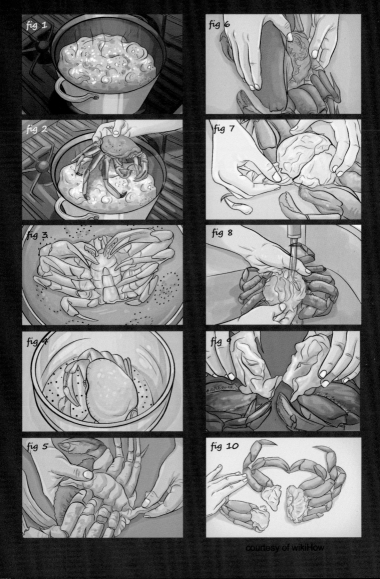

fig 1

fig 6

fig 2

fig 7

fig 3

fig 8

fig 4

fig 9

fig 5

fig 10

courtesy of wikiHow

BRIE & CRAB DIP

Serves **4**

2 tablespoons **butter**
1 tablespoon **garlic,** minced
2 tablespoons **shallot,** minced
1 (8-ounce) wheel of **brie cheese,** rind removed and
    cut into half inch pieces
1 (8-ounce) package of **cream cheese,** room temperature
1 cup **heavy whipping cream**
¼ cup **ricotta cheese**
1 cup **crabmeat,** finely chopped
1 teaspoon **lemon juice**
½ teaspoon sea **salt**
¼ teaspoon ground black **pepper**
2 **green apples,** sliced
French bread

In a skillet over medium-low heat, melt the butter and sauté the garlic and shallot until soft.

Add the brie cheese to the skillet and stir frequently. Cut the cream cheese into cubes and add to the skillet along with the whipping cream. Stir frequently until the cheese melts.

Remove from heat and use a rubber spatula to move everything to a mixing bowl. Let mixture cool then add ricotta cheese, crabmeat, lemon juice, salt and pepper. Blend until combined.

Preheat your oven to 400°F. Transfer the mixture directly to oven-proof ramekins or a baking dish. Bake for 10 to 15 minutes or until lightly browned. Serve the dip with slices of apple and French bread.

A Note from LaDonna Rose
After testing several crab dip recipes that were a hit and miss, I made it my mission to find the perfect recipe for this book. My friend Michael Briggs gave me this recipe and it was an instant hit! If you've never had crab dip before, I hope you enjoy it as much as we do!

Jumbo Lump Crab Cocktail

Makes **4**

Cocktail Sauce
1 teaspoon **wasabi**
1 cup **ketchup**
1 tablespoon prepared **horseradish**
2 tablespoons **lemon juice**
1 teaspoon **Worcestershire sauce**

Crostinis
4 tablespoons **butter**
1 tablespoon **garlic,** minced
1 French **baguette bread**

Crabmeat
2 cups **crabmeat**
grated zest of 1 **lemon**
1 **dill** sprig

Cocktail Sauce: In a small bowl, combine all cocktail sauce ingredients and mix well. Set aside.

Preheat your oven to 325˚F.

Crostinis: Melt butter with garlic in a small pan. Cut the baguette into 16 round slices and brush both sides with garlic butter. Place the coated bread rounds in a single layer on a rimmed baking sheet and bake in the oven until lightly toeasted. Set aside.

Using small glasses, place two tablespoons of the cocktail sauce at the bottom of each. Add a half cup of crabmeat on top of the cocktail sauce in each glass. Garnish with lemon zest and a bit of dill. Serve chilled with the crostinis.

CRAB STUFFED MUSHROOMS

Makes **24**

3 slices quality **bacon,** cooked, diced
24 medium-sized **mushroom caps,** hollowed
2 cups **crabmeat,** finely chopped
⅓ cup **cream cheese,** softened
¼ cup **heavy cream**
1 tablespoon **garlic,** minced
1 **shallot,** minced
1½ cups **baby spinach,** chopped
4 tablespoons **Parmesan cheese,** finely grated
1 teaspoon **lemon juice**
1 teaspoon **Worcestershire sauce**
⅛ teaspoon **Siracha hot sauce**
sea **salt** and freshly ground black **pepper,** to taste
½ cup fresh **bread crumbs,** crust removed and cut into ¼-inch cubes
2 tablespoons **olive oil**
3 tablespoons **Parmesan cheese,** finely grated
sea **salt** and freshly ground black **pepper**

Preheat your oven to 425°F. Place mushroom caps, hollow side up, on a rimmed baking sheet that has been lined with parchment paper.

In a medium bowl, combine cream cheese and heavy cream. Add garlic, shallots, spinach, 4 tablespoons Parmesan, lemon juice, Worcestershire and hot sauce. Season with salt and pepper. Gently stir in diced bacon and crabmeat.

In a small bowl, toss bread crumbs with the olive oil, 3 tablespoons Parmesan, salt and pepper to taste.

Stuff mushrooms by dividing crab filling evenly into each cap. Top with the crumbs, pressing lightly. Bake 8 to 10 minutes until heated through and topping is golden. Serve immediately.

CRAB RANGOON

Makes **32** Wontons

½ cup **cream cheese,** softened
1 tablespoon fresh **cilantro,** minced
2 teaspoons **green onions,** minced
1 teaspoon fresh **ginger,** minced
1 teaspoon **sugar**
1 teaspoon **jalapeño,** seeded, minced
1 tablespoon **lime juice**
1 cup **crabmeat**
32 **wonton wrappers**
1 cup **vegetable oil**
sweet & savory sauce for serving, page 66

Blend cream cheese, cilantro, green onions, ginger, sugar, jalapeño and lime juice in a bowl; gently fold in the crabmeat.

Arrange wonton wrappers on a work surface. Place 1 teaspoon of crab mixture in the center of each, then moisten edges with water. Fold to form a triangle, pressing to seal. Moisten the outer corners of the triangle, seal together to form a "hat" and place on a parchment-lined baking sheet. Heat oil to 350˚ degrees in a heavy bottomed pan over medium-high heat.

Carefully fry wontons in batches until golden on both sides, 2-3 minutes total. Drain on paper towels; fry remaining wontons in the same way.

Serve with sweet & savory sauce, if desired.

CRAB SAUTÉ

Makes **2** servings
3 tablespoons **butter**
2 teaspoons **garlic,** minced
¼ cup **white wine**
1½ cups **crabmeat** (if using king or snow, cut into bite-size pieces)
½ teaspoon ground black **pepper**
¼ cup **green onions,** chopped
1 tablespoon **lemon juice**
French **baguette bread,** cut into ½-inch slices
olive oil
¼ cup **Parmesan cheese,** shredded

In a saucepan, heat butter over medium heat. Add garlic, wine and crab. Stir in pepper, green onions and lemon juice. Cook until crab mixture is heated through.

Meanwhile, preheat broiler.

Arrange bread slices in a single layer on a rimmed baking sheet; brush top of each slice with olive oil and sprinkle with Parmesan. Place under the broiler until the tops are brown and bread is crisp.

Spoon crab mixture over grilled bread. Serve immediately.

tidbits:
There are three guaranteed triggers for seasickness: going below for any length of time, looking through binoculars for anything longer than a glance and trying to read a book. For me, ginger is a good natural alternative for seasickness. Nimble on candied ginger or make a tea with ground ginger, adding 1 teaspoon to a mug of boiling water and letting it steep for a few minutes, adding honey to taste.

Soft Spring Rolls with Crab

Makes **10-12**

3 ounces **thin rice noodles, cooked**
12 round **rice paper sheets**
1½ cups **crabmeat** (if using king or snow, slice into small strips)
1 large **avocado,** sliced into strips
2 cups **red cabbage,** shredded
2 cups **carrot,** shredded
½ cup **cilantro** leaves
½ cup **mint** leaves
½ cup **basil** leaves
6 **green onions,** cut into thin strips

Peanut Dipping Sauce
⅓ cup **creamy peanut butter**
1 tablespoon low-sodium **soy sauce**
2 tablespoons **hoisin sauce**
2 teaspoons **Siracha hot sauce**
1 teaspoon **ginger,** grated
6 tablespoons **hot water,** to thin

Peanut Dipping Sauce: In a bowl, mix together the sauce ingredients until smooth. Set aside.

Arrange all the ingredients separately around a large cutting board or tray set before you. Set out a platter to hold the finished rolls, as well as a large shallow bowl filled with very warm water.

To make each roll, slide one sheet of rice paper into the pan of warm water and press gently to submerge it for about 10 seconds. Remove it carefully, draining the water and place it before you on the cutting board.

Line up a horizontal row of each of the following ingredients on the rice paper sheet, starting on the lowest third of the sheet and working away from you: a small amount of crabmeat, a tangle of noodles, a few avocado slices, a row of cabbage and carrots, a row of cilantro, mint and basil and a row of green onion slivers on top.

Fold the bottom half of the wrapper over the filling, hold the filling in place, tuck in the sides and roll tightly. Repeat with the remaining filling and serve with the dipping sauce.

CRAB CAKES

Makes **8-10**

4 cups **crabmeat**
½ cup **mayonnaise**
½ cup fresh **parsley,** chopped
1 tablespoon **garlic,** minced
¼ cup **lemon juice**
1 large **egg**
2 teaspoons Dijon **mustard**
1 tablespoon **Old Bay seasoning**
1 cup Panko **bread crumbs,** plus ½ to ¾ cup for forming
⅛ cup **sesame seeds**
olive oil or peanut oil for frying
tartar sauce for serving, page 67

In a large bowl, combine all ingredients, (except sesame seeds and oil) stirring gently to combine. Dividing evenly, form mixture into 8 to 10 cakes Dredge each mound in Panko and sesame seeds to coat, set aside.

In a large nonstick skillet over medium-high heat; sauté half of the cakes in 1½ tablespoons of oil. Cook until golden, about 3 minutes, then carefully flip the cakes over and cook on the other side about 2 minutes more. Transfer to a paper-towel-lined plate. Sauté remaining cakes in the same manner. Serve with tartar sauce, if desired.

CROSTINI WITH AVOCADO & CRAB

Makes **12**
1 French **baguette bread,** cut into ½-inch slices
2 tablespoons **olive oil**
1 large ripe **avocado**
2 teaspoons **garlic,** minced
1 tablespoon **shallot,** minced
2 tablespoons **lime juice,** divided
½ teaspoon sea **salt,** divided
1 cup **crabmeat** (if using king or snow, cut into bite-size pieces)
⅛ teaspoon **red pepper flakes**

Preheat your oven to 375˚F. Arrange bread slices in a single layer on a rimmed baking sheet; brush top of each slice with olive oil. Bake 8 to 10 minutes or until lightly toasted.

In a medium bowl, mash the avocado using the back of a fork. Add garlic, shallot, 1 tablespoon lime juice and salt; stir well to combine.

In a medium bowl, combine crabmeat, red pepper and remaining 1 tablespoon lime juice. Toss gently to combine.

Spread avocado mixture evenly over toasts. Top evenly with crab mixture and serve.

CRAB CROQUETTES

Makes **18-20**
<u>Croquettes</u>
2 cups **crabmeat**
1 cup Panko **bread crumbs**
¼ cup **green onions,** minced
1 tablespoon fresh **parsley,** minced
2 tablespoons grated **lemon zest**
2 tablespoons **lemon juice**
⅓ cup **mayonnaise**
1¼ teaspoons **Old Bay seasoning**
1 teaspoon **Worcestershire** sauce
¼ teaspoon ground **cayenne**
½ teaspoon ground **mustard**

<u>Batter</u>
4 **egg yolks**
½ cup **milk**
½ cup **cold club soda** or beer
2¼ teaspoons **Old Bay seasoning**
1 cup all-purpose **flour**
2 teaspoons **baking powder**
vegetable oil (about 4 cups) for frying
sweet and savory sauce for serving, page 66

Croquettes: In a large bowl, gently combine crabmeat through mustard. **Batter:** In a small bowl, whisk together egg yolks, milk, club soda and Old Bay. Add the flour and baking powder and gently stir until batter is just combined.

Heat 2-inches oil in a 3-quart straight-sided heavy bottomed pan over medium heat until it reaches 350˚ degrees on a deep-fat thermometer.

Form crab mixture into "cocktail size" balls. (About one slightly heaping tablespoon each). Place the crab ball on a slotted spoon and coat with the batter. (Let the excess batter drain off). Carefully lay them into the hot oil. Turn the croquettes frequently until golden brown. Remove croquettes to a paper-towel-lined plate. Serve immediately with the sweet and savory sauce, if desired.

CRAB LOUIS WONTON CUPS

Makes **24**

24 **wonton wrappers**
¼ cup **mayonnaise**
¼ cup **cream cheese,** softened
2 tablespoons **ketchup**
2 teaspoons **Siracha hot sauce**
1 teaspoon **Worcestershire sauce**
1½ cups **crabmeat**
½ cup **green bell pepper,** diced
¼ cup **green onions,** chopped
2 teaspoons grated **lemon zest,** minced
⅛ teaspoon sea **salt**
pinch ground black **pepper**
grape tomato slices, for garnish
strips of **lemon zest,** for garnish

Preheat your oven to 325°F.

Lightly grease 24 mini muffin cups. Place center of wonton wrappers in the wells of prepared pan to form a cup, allowing remainder of wrapper to extend above the pan. Bake in the oven 8 minutes or until crisp and lightly brown.

In a bowl, combine mayonnaise, cream cheese, ketchup, hot sauce and Worcestershire. Fold in the crabmeat, bell pepper, green onions and lemon zest; season with salt and pepper. Fill wonton cups with crab mixture.

Garnish with tomatoes and strips of lemon zest.

A Note from LaDonna Rose
Alternately, this simple crab mixture, sparked by just a couple seasonings can be heaped onto crisp hollowed cucumber rounds. I make this very often every summer because, to my mind, it is everything an hors d'oeuvre should be - full of rich flavor yet not so heavy as to spoil the course to come.

MINI CRAB QUICHES

Makes **12**

1½ cups **cream cheese,** softened
1½ cups **Parmesan cheese,** finely shredded, divided
2 **eggs**
¼ cup **green onions,** minced
½ teaspoon **Old Bay seasoning**
¼ teaspoon sea **salt**
⅛ teaspoon **cayenne pepper**
1½ cups **crabmeat**
1½ cups Panko **bread crumbs**
⅓ cup **butter,** melted
sweet and savory sauce for serving, page 66

Using a hand or stand mixer, beat the cream cheese on medium speed until well blended. Add ¾ cup of the Parmesan, eggs, green onions, Old Bay, salt and cayenne pepper. Beat on medium speed until smooth. Fold in crabmeat. Cover and chill for 1 hour.

Preheat your oven to 350˚F. Coat twelve 2½-inch muffin cups with nonstick cooking spray. In a small bowl, combine the remaining ¾ cup Parmesan, bread crumbs and the melted butter.

Place 1 tablespoon of the bread crumb mixture in the bottom of each muffin cup. Divide the crab mixture among the muffin cups, pressing gently to flatten. Top each with the remaining bread crumb mixture, pressing lightly to adhere.

Bake for 30 to 35 minutes until golden. Remove from oven and let cool for 5 minutes before serving. Gently remove crab quiches from muffin cups. For a tasty treat, serve with the sweet and savory sauce.

CRAB SALAD ON CORN BLINI

Makes **12-16**

1½ cups **crabmeat**
¼ cup **red bell pepper,** finely chopped
2 tablespoons **chives,** minced
1½ teaspoons **Dijon** mustard
1½ tablespoons **mayonnaise,** divided
½ teaspoon sea **salt,** divided
¼ teaspoon ground black **pepper**
1 **avocado,** pit removed
2 tablespoons **lime juice**
1 small **jalapeño,** cut in half lengthwise, seeded and thinly sliced, divided
Corn Blini
1 teaspoon RapidRise **yeast**
2 tablespoons **warm water** (120˚)
½ cup yellow **cornmeal**
½ cup all-purpose **flour**
¼ teaspoon sea **salt**
½ cup 2% **milk**
3 tablespoons **butter,** melted

In a medium bowl, gently toss the crabmeat, bell pepper, chives, Dijon, 1 tablespoon mayonnaise, ¼ teaspoon salt and pepper until combined. Refrigerate. In the bowl of a small food processor, combine the avocado, remaining mayonnaise, lime juice, half the jalapeño slices, remaining salt and pulse until the mixture is smooth.

Corn Blini: In a small bowl, combine the yeast and water and let stand until foamy, about 5 minutes. In a medium bowl, stir together the cornmeal, flour and salt. Add the milk, butter and yeast mixture, whisking until smooth. Let the mixture sit uncovered, at room temperature for 10 minutes.

Heat a nonstick skillet over medium heat; when hot, spray the pan with nonstick cooking spray. Working in batches of three, spoon 1 tablespoon batter into skillet for each blini and cook 2 to 3 minutes on each side until crisp around the edges and golden brown. Transfer to a plate and cover with foil to keep them warm. Top each blini with crab salad; garnish with avocado purée and remaining jalapeño slices, if desired.

32

BRUNCH & LUNCH

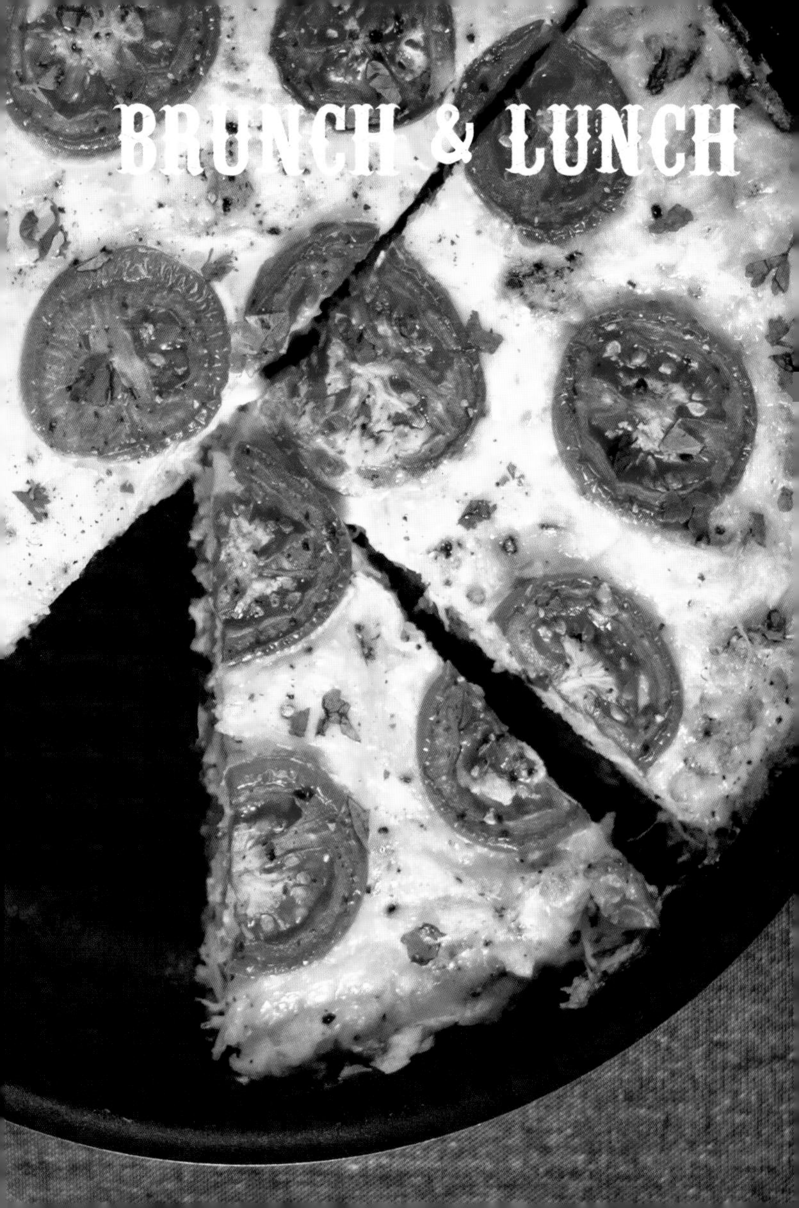

CRAB STRATA

Serves **6**

4 slices thick-cut **bacon, cooked** and chopped
2 cups **mushrooms,** sliced
6 slices **French bread**
¼ cup **butter,** softened, divided
6 large **eggs**
1 cup **half-and-half**
½ teaspoon sea **salt**
¼ teaspoon ground black **pepper**
1½ cups **Mozzarella cheese,** grated
1½ cups **crabmeat** (if using king or snow, cut into bite-size pieces)
½ cup **green onions,** chopped
2 tablespoons fresh **parsley,** chopped, for garnish

Butter a 7 x 11-inch baking dish; set aside.

Melt 1 tablespoon butter in a skillet over medium-high heat. Add the mushrooms, sauté until soft. Let cool.

Butter bread on one side, stack the bread and cut into small cubes. In a medium bowl, whisk together eggs, half-and-half, salt and pepper.

Layer one half of the bread in the prepared pan, one half of the cheese, crabmeat, onions, bacon and mushrooms. Repeat layers.

Pour egg mixture over layers and garnish with parsley. Cover and refrigerate one hour or up to overnight.

Remove Strata from refrigerator 30 minutes before baking (if prepared the night before) and preheat your oven to 350˚F. Bake uncovered until puffed and golden and a toothpick inserted near the center comes out clean, 45-60 minutes.

FRITTATA WITH CRAB & CHORIZO

Serves **4**

2 tablespoons **olive oil**
1 cup **chorizo sausage** (or kielbasa, cut into bite-size pieces)
2 cups **sweet potato,** shredded
½ cup sliced **yellow bell pepper**
¼ cup yellow **onion,** diced
8 **eggs**
1 tablespoon **milk**
½ teaspoon sea **salt**
¼ teaspoon ground black **pepper**
1 cup **crabmeat** (if using king or snow, cut into bite-size pieces)
½ cup **Monterey Jack cheese**
2 Roma or Vine **tomatoes,** sliced
cilantro, for garnish

Preheat your oven to 350°F. Heat the oil in an oven-safe skillet over medium heat. Add sausage, sweet potato, yellow pepper and onion and sauté for a few minutes.

Beat the eggs with the milk and salt then pour into the skillet and cook for 2 minutes. Scatter the crabmeat and cheese over the eggs. Arrange the tomato slices in a circular pattern on top of the eggs. Place the frittata in the oven and bake for 20 minutes or until eggs test done.

Garnish with cilantro and serve.

A Note from LaDonna Rose
I'm a little obsessed with frittata's, which is the perfect make ahead boat food. It uses up leftovers, it can be made with many different ingredients, transports easily and contains no pastry-a bonus in this healthy age. Serve it with a crunchy green salad and a crisp white wine and that's one outstanding boat lunch.

CRAB EGGS BENEDICT

Serves **4**

<u>Crab Cakes</u>
4 cups **crabmeat**
½ cup **mayonnaise**
½ cup fresh **parsley,** chopped
4 **garlic** cloves, minced
¼ cup **lemon juice**
1 large **egg**
2 tablespoons Dijon **mustard**
1 tablespoon **Old Bay seasoning**
1 cup Panko **bread crumbs,** plus ½ to ¾ cup for forming
⅛ cup **sesame seeds**
olive oil or peanut oil for frying

<u>Hollandaise Sauce</u>
1 tablespoon **mayonnaise** or 1 egg yolk
½ teaspoon Dijon **mustard**
1½ teaspoons **lemon juice**
½ cup **butter,** melted
sea **salt** and ground black **pepper,** to taste
1 teaspoon **white vinegar**
6 large **eggs**
4 **English muffins,** split and toasted
lemon wedges for serving

Crab Cakes: In a large bowl combine all ingredients, (except sesame seeds and oil) stirring gently to combine. Dividing evenly, form mixture into 8 cakes. Dredge each mound in Panko and sesame seeds to coat, set aside.

In a large non-stick skillet over medium-high heat sauté half the cakes in 1½ tablespoons of oil. Cook until golden, about 3 minutes, then carefully flip the cakes over and cook on the other side about 2 minutes more. Transfer to a paper-towel-lined-plate. Sauté remaining cakes in the same manner.

Hollandaise Sauce: In a blender, (or whisk by hand) place mayonnaise (or egg), mustard and lemon juice; whirl at high speed until blended. With blender running, add melted butter a few drops at a time, then increase flow to a steady stream. Season with salt and pepper.

Poached Eggs: Fill a large skillet with enough water to reach a depth of 1 1/2-inches and bring to a boil. Add the vinegar and heat until bubbles form on the pan bottom with an occasional one popping to the top. Break each egg into the water; do not overcrowd. Cook until set to your liking (poke white gently to check for firmness). For soft yolks and firm whites, allow 3 minutes.

To Assemble: Place two English muffin halves on each of 4 plates. Divide crab cakes among the muffins and top each with a poached egg and some sauce.

RUSTIC CRAB QUICHE

Serves **4**

1 (9-inch) frozen **deep dish pie shell**, thawed
4 large **eggs**
2 cups **heavy cream**
2 tablespoons fresh **chives**, plus whole chives for topping
2 tablespoons fresh **parsley**, chopped
1 tablespoon **lemon zest**
½ teaspoon **Old Bay seasoning**
½ teaspoon sea **salt**
¼ teaspoon ground black **pepper**
⅛ teaspoon ground **nutmeg**
¾ cup Monterey **Jack cheese**, grated
¾ cup **Swiss cheese**, grated
1 cup **crabmeat** (if using king or snow, cut into bite-size pieces)

Preheat your oven to 375°F. Prick bottom of pie dough with a fork to prevent fluffing while baking. Bake until pie crust is golden brown, about 15 minutes. Let cool completely. Reduce oven temperature to 350°F.

In a medium bowl, whisk together eggs, cream, chives, parsley, lemon zest, Old Bay, salt, pepper and nutmeg. Set aside.

Evenly sprinkle cheese into prebaked crust. Arrange crabmeat evenly over cheese. Pour egg mixture over crabmeat and cheese. Lay several whole chives across the top.

Bake until quiche is set and slightly puffed, 40-50 minutes. Let cool 15 minutes before serving.

CRAB STRUDEL

Serves **4**

1 frozen **puff pastry** sheet, thawed
8 **eggs**
½ cup **milk**
¼ teaspoon sea **salt**
¼ teaspoon black **pepper**
2 tablespoons butter, softened
4 ounces **cream cheese,** softened
2 tablespoons **green onions,** minced
1 teaspoon fresh **dill,** chopped
1 cup **crabmeat** (if using king or snow, cut into bite-size pieces)
⅓ cup **Mozzarella cheese,** grated
1 **egg,** slightly beaten
1 tablespoon **water**

Preheat your oven to 350°F. Line a baking sheet with parchment paper, set aside. Whisk the eggs in a medium bowl until well blended, add the milk salt and pepper.

In a large skillet, melt butter over medium heat, pour in the egg mixture. Cook without stirring until mixture begins to set on the bottom and around the edges. Using a spatula, lift and fold the partially cooked eggs so the uncooked portion flows underneath. Continue cooking until eggs are just set. Remove from heat. Dot with cream cheese and sprinkle with green onions and dill. Stir gently until combined.

Unfold pastry on a lightly floured surface. Roll into a 15 x 12-inch rectangle. Place on baking sheet. Arrange the crabmeat crosswise down the center ⅓ of the pastry, to within 1-inch of the top and bottom. Spoon the eggs over the crabmeat and sprinkle with the Mozzarella cheese.

Combine the beaten egg with water. Brush the edges of the pastry with the egg mixture. Fold one short side of the pastry overfilling. Fold remaining short side over top. Seal top and ends well and brush the top of the pastry with the egg mixture. Bake 25 minutes or until pastry is a lightly-golden brown.

CRAB DELIGHT

Makes **2**

2 thick slices of **French bread,** cut on the diagonal
3 tablespoons **butter,** melted
⅓ cup **Thousand Island dressing, page 43**
1 cup **crabmeat** (if using king or snow, cut into bite-sized pieces)
4 large slices **Swiss cheese**

Butter bread and place butter side down in a large nonstick skillet. Spread dressing on each slice. Place crabmeat on top of dressing. Cover with cheese. Grill over low heat until heated through and cheese is melted. You can use a small loaf pan to cover the sandwich while grilling to help melt the cheese.

Snapping a...

*Courtesy of
Ray Troll*

"SHELLFIE"

Ray Troll

GRILLED CRAB REUBEN

Makes **4**

Thousand Island Dressing
½ cup **mayonnaise**
1 tablespoon **sweet relish**
1 tablespoon **ketchup**
Stir all in a bowl until well blended.

8 slices **Russian rye bread**
8 slices **Swiss cheese,** more if needed
2 cups **crabmeat** (if using king or snow, cut into bite-size pieces)
2 cups **sauerkraut,** drained
¼ cup **butter,** softened, more if needed
4 slices **dill pickle**

Arrange the bread slices on a work surface and spread a little of the dressing on each slice. Put a slice of cheese on each piece of bread; divide the crabmeat among 4 of the slices, then top each with the sauerkraut.

Invert the remaining cheese-covered bread slices onto each sandwich and spread butter on the top of each. Melt the remaining butter in a large nonstick skillet over medium heat. Arrange the sandwiches, butter-side up in the pan and grill each side until toasty and cheese is melted. Top with a sliced pickle.

CARMELIZED GARLIC & CRAB TART

Serves **4**

1 frozen **puff pastry sheet,** thawed in the refrigerator
3 heads of garlic, cloves separated and peeled
1 tablespoon **olive oil**
1 tablespoon **balsamic vinegar**
1 cup **water**
1 tablespoon **sugar**
1 tablespoon fresh **rosemary,** chopped
2 teaspoons fresh **thyme,** chopped, plus 2 sprigs for garnish
¼ teaspoon sea **salt**
4½ ounces **soft, creamy goat cheese,** break into pieces
4½ ounces **hard, goat cheese,** grated
1 cup **crabmeat,** finely chopped
2 **eggs**
⅓ cup **heavy cream** and ⅓ cup **sour cream**
½ teaspoon sea **salt** and ¼ teaspoon ground black **pepper**
1 (11-inch) **tart pan,** with a removable bottom

Preheat your oven to 350˚F. Roll out the pastry into a circle slightly larger than the tart pan. Press it into the pan, allowing it to drape over the side. Place a circle of waxed paper on the bottom and fill with dried beans. Bake the shell for 15 minutes. Remove the beans and paper, bake for 10 minutes more. Remove from oven. Reduce your oven temperature to 325˚F.

While the tart shell is baking, make the caramelized garlic. Put the cloves, in a small saucepan and cover with water. Bring to a simmer and blanch for 2 minutes; drain. Place the cloves and olive oil back in the same pan and sauté over medium-high heat. Add the vinegar and water and bring to a boil. Reduce heat and simmer for 10 minutes. Add the sugar, rosemary, thyme and ¼ tsp. salt. Continue simmering for 10 minutes more.

Assemble Tart: Scatter both types of goat cheese into the bottom of the shell. Scatter crabmeat over the cheese. Spoon in the garlic and syrup. **In a small bowl,** whisk together the eggs, cream, sour cream, salt and pepper. Pour this over the garlic. Bake the tart for 35 to 45 minutes or until the filling has set and the top is golden. Remove from oven and let cool for 10 minutes. Take out of the pan and garnish with a few sprigs of thyme and serve.

CRAB LOUIE SANDWICH

Makes **4**

4 slices **bacon, cooked**
⅓ cup **mayonnaise**
1 teaspoon grated **lemon zest**
1 tablespoon fresh **lemon juice**
2 tablespoons **ketchup**
1 tablespoon **horseradish**
2 tablespoons **green onions,** thinly sliced
½ cup **celery,** diced
½ cup **red bell pepper,** diced
2 cups **crabmeat**
⅛ teaspoon sea **salt**
⅛ teaspoon ground black **pepper**

4 soft **sandwich rolls,** halved, buttered and toasted
lettuce leaves
1 medium **avocado,** thinly sliced

In a medium bowl, whisk together the mayonnaise, lemon zest, lemon juice, ketchup and horseradish. Fold in the green onions, celery, bell pepper, crabmeat, salt and pepper. Place lettuce on the bottom of each roll. Top with crab salad, avocado slices, bacon and the roll top.

MARGARITA CRAB PIZZA

Makes **2**

1 package Rapid Rise **yeast**
1½ teaspoon **sugar**
½ cup **lukewarm water** (105°to 115°)
4 tablespoons **olive oil,** divided
2 cups **all-purpose flour,** divided
1 teaspoon sea **salt**
2 tablespoons **garlic,** minced
½ cup **Parmesan cheese,** grated
1 cup **crabmeat** (if using king or snow, cut into bite-size pieces)
1½ cups **tomatoes,** seeded, diced
1 cup **Mozzarella cheese,** grated
2 teaspoons **Italian seasoning**
fresh basil leaves

In a large bowl, mix the yeast and sugar into the water. Let stand 5 minutes; stir in 2 tablespoons olive oil. Add 1½ cups flour, then salt.

On a lightly floured work surface **(using remaining ½ cup flour)**, knead dough for 5 minutes; divide into two balls. Cover dough with a tea towel and let rest for 10 minutes; punch down into two flat disks.

Preheat your oven to 450°F. Beginning at the center, press balls of dough into 8-inch rounds with raised edges. Line a large baking sheet with parchment paper and place the two rounds of dough on the baking sheet. Brush each round with 1 tablespoon olive oil; sprinkle half of the garlic and half of the Parmesan cheese on each round. Evenly scatter half of the crabmeat, tomatoes and a half of the Mozzarella over each pie. Lightly drizzle additional olive oil over the cheese and sprinkle with Italian seasoning.

Bake until crust and cheese are lightly browned, about 15 minutes. Scatter with basil; let rest 5 minutes, then cut into wedges.

CRAB BLT SANDWICH

Makes **2**

4 strips thick-sliced **bacon, cooked**
4 slices **Texas toast,** buttered and toasted on one side
⅓ cup **mayonnaise**
1 teaspoon grated **lemon zest**
1 tablespoon fresh **lemon juice**
1½ teaspoons **Old Bay seasoning**
2 tablespoons **green onions,** minced
¼ cup **celery,** diced
½ cup **red bell pepper,** diced
2 tablespoons fresh **basil,** chopped
1 cup **crabmeat**
green leaf **lettuce**
4 thin **tomato slices**
1 small **avocado,** thinly sliced

In a medium bowl, whisk together mayonnaise, lemon zest, lemon juice, Old Bay, green onions, celery, bell pepper and basil. Gently fold in crabmeat, being careful not to break it up too much.

Assemble sandwiches by layering lettuce on two slices of bread, then top each with crab salad, two slices of tomato, avocado slices and two strips of bacon. Top each with another slice of bread, toasted side up.

> **tidbits:**
> **How to read a barometer:** Every boat should have a barometer. The rule of thumb is that the higher the pressure the more settled the weather and vice versa.
> **Falling steadily:** Bad weather on the way.
> **Rising steadily:** Good weather on the way.
> **Falling rapidly:** Bad weather and gales coming soon.
> **Rising rapidly:** Better weather, though it may be short-lived.

CRAB CAKE PO' BOY

Makes **4**

¼ cup **mayonnaise**
1 large **egg**
1½ teaspoons **Old Bay seasoning**
1 teaspoon **garlic,** minced
2 tablespoons **lemon juice**
1 teaspoon Dijon **mustard**
2 cups **crabmeat**
1 cup Panko **bread crumbs,** divided
⅓ cup **red bell pepper,** diced
⅓ cup **green onions,** minced
½ cup **Mozzarella cheese,** grated
olive oil for frying
4 **hoagie buns,** buttered and lightly toasted
shredded lettuce
tartar sauce, page 67

In a large bowl, whisk mayonnaise, egg, Old Bay, garlic, lemon juice and Dijon.

Gently add crabmeat, ½ cup bread crumbs, bell pepper, green onions and Mozzarella cheese.

Dividing evenly, form mixture into 12 cakes. Dredge each mound in bread crumbs and transfer to a baking sheet. Chill for 30 minutes.

Heat a nonstick skillet over medium-high heat. Add 2 tablespoons oil to the pan. When hot, add the cakes and cook until golden, 3-4 minutes per side, then drain on paper towels.

Arrange 3 cakes on each toasted bun, top with lettuce and tartar sauce.

SOUPS & SALADS

POTATO-FENNEL CRAB SOUP

Serves **4**

1½ cups **crabmeat**
½ cup fresh **parsley,** chopped, divided
½ cup fresh **basil,** chopped, divided
2 teaspoons grated **lemon zest,** divided
¼ cup **lemon juice,** divided
⅛ teaspoon sea **salt** and ⅛ teaspoon ground black **pepper**
3 tablespoons **olive oil**
4 (½-inch thick) slices **French bread,** cubed
2 tablespoons **butter**
1 bunch **leeks,** chopped
2 cups **Yukon gold potatoes,** peeled and chopped
1 **fennel bulb,** cored and chopped
½ cup dry **white wine** or chicken broth
½ cup **heavy cream**

In a bowl, toss the crabmeat, with 2 Tbls. parsley, 2 Tbls. basil, 1 tsp. lemon zest, 2 Tbls. lemon juice, salt and pepper. Cover and refrigerate. **Preheat** your oven to 350˚F. In a separate bowl; whisk remaining lemon zest, lemon juice and the olive oil. Toss 1 Tbl. of the lemon oil with the bread cubes. Spread the bread cubes in a single layer on a rimmed baking sheet and sprinkle with a little salt and pepper. Bake 15 minutes or until croutons are golden, stirring once. Set aside.

In a soup pot, over medium heat; melt butter. Add the leeks and sauté until soft. Stir in the potatoes and fennel. Cover and cook about 10 minutes or until the potatoes are nearly tender. Stir in the wine, 1½ tsps. salt and ¼ tsp. pepper. Stir in 5 cups water, ¼ cup parsley and ¼ cup basil and bring slowly to a boil. Reduce heat to low, cover and simmer 20 minutes or until the potatoes are nearly tender. Working in small batches, purée the soup in a blender (or use a stick blender and puree the soup right in the cooking pot). Return the soup to the pot, add the cream and bring to a simmer. Stir in the remaining parsley and basil and season with salt and pepper. Ladle the soup into bowls and top with the crabmeat, croutons and drizzle each with the remaining lemon oil.

Avocado-Crab & Tomato Towers

Makes **8**

1½ cups **crabmeat**
2 tablespoons **mayonnaise**
1 tablespoon fresh **dill,** chopped, plus sprigs for garnish
1 tablespoon fresh **parsley,** chopped
2 teaspoons grated **lemon zest**
½ teaspoon sea **salt,** divided
¼ teaspoon ground black **pepper,** divided
2 ripe **avocados,** diced
2 tablespoons fresh **lemon juice**
8 **cherry tomatoes,** sliced ⅛-inch thick

In a medium bowl, combine crabmeat, mayonnaise, dill, parsley, lemon zest, ¼ teaspoon salt and ⅛ teaspoon pepper.

In a small bowl, combine avocado, lemon juice, remaining ¼ teaspoon salt and ⅛ teaspoon pepper.

Place a 3½-inch ring mold on the center of a small serving plate. Gently press about 2 tablespoons avocado into the bottom. Press about 2 tablespoons crab mixture on top of the avocado. Carefully remove ring mold. Top with sliced tomatoes. Repeat with remaining avocado, crab mixture, and tomatoes. Serve immediately.

> **tidbits:**
> The name "Dungeness" comes from one of the most fertile habitats of this species: The Dungeness Spit, a sandy stretch of land in Northwest Washington. The spit and surrounding community is located on the Strait of Jaun de Fuca and named after a desert-like beach of the same name in England.

SPICY CRAB VEGGIE SOUP

Serves **4**

4 slices quality-thick cut **bacon,** chopped
1 cup **onion,** diced
1½ cups **Yukon gold potatoes,** peeled, diced
1 tablespoon **jalapeño,** seeded, diced
1 tablespoon **garlic,** minced
2 cups **tomatoes,** chopped
½ teaspoon sea **salt**
¼ teaspoon ground black **pepper**
¼ teaspoon **red pepper flakes**
1 teaspoon dried **thyme**
4 cups organic **chicken broth**
4 cups fresh baby **spinach,** chopped
1 (14-ounce) can **coconut milk**
2 cups lump **crabmeat** (if using king or snow, cut into bite-size pieces)
2 tablespoons **lime juice,** plus more to taste
½ cup **green onions,** chopped

In a soup pot; fry the bacon until crisp. Using a slotted spoon, transfer to paper towels to drain. Pour off all but 1 tablespoon drippings.

Stir in the onion, potatoes, jalapeño and garlic. Add the tomatoes and seasonings and cook over medium heat, stirring often, until the onions are soft.

Stir in the chicken broth and bring to a slow boil. Cover and simmer 10 minutes or until the potatoes are nearly tender. Gently stir in the spinach, coconut milk, crabmeat, lime juice and reserved bacon.

Ladle into warmed soup bowls and garnish with the green onions.

CRAB CURRY SOUP

Serves **4**

1 tablespoon **olive oil**
1 medium **onion,** thinly sliced
1 tablespoon **garlic,** minced
2 tablespoons **green curry paste**
8 cups organic **chicken broth**
1 (14-ounce) can **coconut milk**
2 tablespoons **fish sauce,** plus more to taste
2 **red bell peppers,** thinly sliced
6 ounces thin **rice noodles,** broken into pieces
2 cups **crabmeat** (if using king or snow, cut into bite-size pieces)
2 tablespoons **lime juice,** plus more to taste
1 cup **cilantro,** chopped

Heat the oil in a soup pot over medium-high heat. Add the onion and sauté until softened. Add the garlic and curry paste and cook, stirring, 1 to 2 minutes. Stir in the coconut milk and fish sauce; cover and bring to a slow boil. **Add** the bell peppers and noodles and simmer, uncovered, until the noodles are al dente, about 3 minutes. Gently add the crabmeat and stir in the lime juice and cilantro. Add more fish sauce and lime juice, if desired. Serve warm.

CRAB CORN CHOWDER

Serves **4**
3 tablespoons **butter**
1 medium **onion,** chopped
1 stalk **celery,** chopped
1 medium **carrot,** grated
1 tablespoon **garlic,** minced
3 cups **Yukon gold potatoes,** peeled and diced
4 cups organic **chicken broth**
¼ teaspoon sea **salt**
¼ teaspoon ground black **pepper**
½ teaspoon **Old Bay seasoning**
2 cups **crabmeat** (if using king or snow, cut into bite-size pieces)
2½ cups **half-and-half**
1 (15-ounce) can **creamed corn**
1 tablespoon fresh **parsley,** minced

In a soup pot; melt the butter over medium heat. Add the onion, celery, carrots and garlic. Sauté until soft. Stir in the potatoes, broth, salt, pepper and Old Bay. Reduce heat to low and add the crabmeat, half-and-half, creamed corn and parsley, simmer gently until hot. Ladle chowder into warm soup bowls and garnish with parsley.

Homemade Crab Salsa

Makes **6 cups**

3 cups **tomatoes,** seeded and diced
1 cup **red onion,** diced
¾ cup frozen **corn kernels,** thawed
1 tablespoon **garlic,** minced
½ cup **green onions,** chopped
½ cup **cilantro,** chopped
2 **limes,** juiced
2 tablespoons **white vinegar**
½ teaspoon ground **cumin**
½ teaspoon sea **salt**
¼ teaspoon ground black **pepper**
2 cups **crabmeat** (if using king or snow, cut into bite-size pieces)
tortilla chips

In a large bowl, toss together the tomatoes, red onion, corn, garlic, onions and cilantro. Add lime juice, vinegar, cumin, salt and pepper. Gently toss in the crabmeat, being careful not to break up the lumps.

Cover and refrigerate until ready to serve.

CRAB LOUIE

Serves **4**

1 head iceburg **lettuce,** torn into pieces
2 cups **crabmeat** (if using king or snow, cut into bite-size pieces)
4 **hard boiled eggs,** chopped or cut into wedges
4 large **radishes,** sliced
2 medium **avocados,** cut into chunks
1 cup **cherry tomatoes,** sliced
½ cup **green onions,** sliced
1 cup **Thousand Island dressing, page 43**

Arrange your salad beautifully on a large platter or in a bowl, passing the dressing at the table.

tidbits:

First things first. To catch Dungeness, you need good bait. We have found that crab love turkey, chicken legs and of course, a fresh fish carcass. Properly secure your bait inside of your crab pot. Once this is done, it's time to catch Dungeness crab like never before!

Crab like somewhat sandy to rocky sea-beds and we find that 55 to 85 feet depth works real well to catch crab. (You will need at least 100 feet of line and a buoy).

Once you've found your "secret crab highway", throw your pot over board! Let the crab pots "soak" for a couple hours, or over night.

Now comes the fun part! Point your boat at your buoy and pull slowly along side of it and grab it out of the water with a gaff hook. Coil your line as it comes on board, this will guard against getting the line all knotted up.

Once you have your crab pot pulled to the surface, pull it into the boat and sort your large haul and measure your catch with a measuring caliper. Throw out all females and juveniles and softer shelled crabs (they won't have much meat in them). It's imperative you keep your crab alive until you are ready to cook them. Have fun!

CRAB-AVOCADO & MANGO QUINOA BOWL

Serves **4**

4 cups **cooked quinoa**
1 cup **crabmeat** (if using king or snow, cut into bite-size pieces)
1 **mango,** chopped
1 large **avocado,** chopped
¼ cup **green onions,** chopped
¼ teaspoon sea **salt**
⅛ teaspoon ground black **pepper**

Lemon-Honey Vinaigrette
⅓ cup **olive oil**
¼ cup fresh **lemon juice**
1 teaspoon **garlic,** minced
1 tablespoon **honey**
sea **salt** and ground black **pepper**

Whisk ingredients for the vinaigrette in a small bowl.

In a large bowl, gently combine cooked quinoa, crabmeat, mango, avocado and green onions. Season with salt and pepper.

Pour the vinaigrette over the quinoa mixture (you may not need all of it), gently toss to coat.

CRAB CAESAR SALAD

Serves **4**

Croutons

4 thick slices **French bread,** crusts removed and cut into ¾-inch cubes
1 tablespoon **olive oil**
2 tablespoons **butter,** melted
3 tablespoons **Parmesan cheese,** grated
2 large **garlic** cloves, minced

Dressing

2 large **garlic** cloves
3 **anchovy fillets**
½ teaspoon **lemon juice**
½ teaspoon Dijon **mustard**
½ teaspoon **Worcestershire sauce**
2 teaspoons **mayonnaise**
⅛ teaspoon sea **salt,** or as needed
¼ teaspoon freshly ground black **pepper**
¼ cup **olive oil**

Salad

1 large head **romaine** lettuce, washed, dried and torn into pieces
½ cup **Parmesan cheese,** grated
freshly ground black **pepper**

2 cups **crabmeat** (if using king or snow, cut into bite-size pieces)

Croutons: Preheat your oven to 350°F. In a large bowl, combine the olive oil and butter. Stir in Parmesan cheese and garlic. Add bread cubes and toss until coated. Spread the bread in a single layer on a shallow rimmed baking sheet and sprinkle with a little salt. Bake until golden, about 15 minutes. Set aside.

Dressing: In a blender, combine the dressing ingredients until smooth.

Salad: In a large salad bowl, combine lettuce and croutons. Pour dressing over lettuce mixture; toss lightly to coat. Add ¼ cup of the Parmesan and toss well.

Divide Caesar salad among four plates and top each with ½ cup of the crabmeat. Garnish with Parmesan and serve.

AVOCADO CRAB BOATS

Serves **2**

2 medium **avocados,** sliced in half length-wise and pitted
¼ cup **red onion,** finely chopped
2 tablespoons **cilantro,** chopped
4 **cherry tomatoes,** diced
3 tablespoons **lime juice**
1 teaspoon **olive oil**
¼ teaspoon sea **salt**
¼ teaspoon ground black **pepper**
1 cup **crabmeat**
4 leaves **butter lettuce,** optional

In a medium bowl, combine onion, cilantro, tomatoes, lime juice, olive oil, salt and pepper. Gently add crabmeat.

Scoop out avocados to create bowls, leaving a small border. Dice scooped out avocado and fold into the crab mixture.

Spoon the mixture equally on top of each avocado half (you may have a little mixture remaining, depending on the size of your avocados). Place on plates with butter lettuce and serve.

Dungeness Crab Legs with Four Sauces

Crab: to Boil or Steam? If you've never cooked live crabs, it can seem intimidating. Here are two methods for getting the critters in the water. Bring a large pot of salted water to a vigorous boil over high heat. Toss in 1 or 2 crabs and boil for 25 minutes. On the other hand... steam them. Add water about 2 inches up the side of a deep pot, then suspend a strainer over the water. Place one or two crabs in the strainer, depending on its size. Cover the pot tightly and steam over high heat for 25 minutes. The crab will be filled, not with water, but with delicious undiluted juices. Make sure to have seafood crackers or small hammers on hand to get at all of the sweet, flaky meat.

Sweet and Savory Sauce

1 tablespoon **butter**
2 teaspoons **garlic,** minced
2 teaspoons fresh **ginger,** grated
1 **jalapeño pepper,** seeded and minced
1 (18-ounce) jar **orange marmalade**
3 tablespoons **lime juice**
1 tablespoon whole-grain **mustard**
1 teaspoon prepared **horseradish**
¼ teaspoon sea **salt**

In a medium saucepan, melt butter over medium-high heat. Add garlic, ginger and jalapeño. Cook for 2 minutes, stirring constantly. Reduce heat to medium-low. Add marmalade, lime juice, mustard, horseradish and salt. Simmer for 5 minutes, stirring frequently. Serve warm.

TARTAR SAUCE

2 cups **mayonnaise**
2 tablespoons **dill pickle relish**
⅓ cup **celery,** minced
⅓ cup **onion,** minced
2 tablespoons **lemon juice**
1 tablespoon **Worcestershire sauce**
⅛ teaspoon ground **mustard**
⅛ teaspoon sea **salt**
⅛ teaspoon ground black **pepper**

Combine all ingredients and mix well.

CLARIFIED GARLIC BUTTER

1 cup **butter** (2 sticks)
2 large cloves **garlic,** minced

Cut butter into pieces and melt slowly in a heavy saucepan over low heat. Simmer gently until foam rises to the top of the melted butter. Remove from heat and skim foam from the surface with a spoon. Pour clarified butter over garlic, into a bowl leaving milky sediment behind. Serve warm.

COCKTAIL SAUCE

1 teaspoon **wasabi**
1 cup **ketchup**
1 tablespoon prepared **horseradish**
2 tablespoons **lemon juice**
1 teaspoon **Worcestershire sauce**
sea **salt** and ground black **pepper**

In a bowl, mix together all ingredients until smooth; add salt and pepper to taste. Let sauce rest (the longer the better) to help release the flavors.

CRAB TACOS

Serves 4

2 cups **crabmeat** (if using king or snow, cut into bite-size pieces)
2 medium **tomatoes,** seeded and diced
1 **avocado,** pit removed and diced
⅓ cup **green onions,** sliced
4 **garlic** cloves, minced
1 **jalapeño** pepper, seeded and minced
¼ cup fresh **basil** leaves, chopped
¼ cup fresh **cilantro,** chopped
⅓ cup **lime juice**
¼ teaspoon sea **salt**
¼ teaspoon freshly ground black **pepper**
8 stone-ground **corn tortillas**
2 cups **Feta cheese,** crumbled

In a large bowl, gently combine crabmeat through black pepper.

When you are ready to serve, heat the tortillas in a dry skillet until just warm and softened, keeping them under a kitchen towel as you go. Place the tortillas on plates, spoon on a layer of the mixture and sprinkle with a little crumbled cheese. The way to eat these is to fold the taco in half and eat by hand; it can get messy, so have plenty of napkins ready to go!

CREAMY CRABMEAT FETTUCCINE

Serves 4

¾ pound **fettuccine,** cooked according to package directions, drain
2 tablespoons **butter**
2 tablespoons **garlic,** chopped
12 button **mushrooms,** quartered
1 (14-ounce) can **artichoke hearts,** halved, drained
¼ cup dry **white wine**
1 pint **heavy cream**
1 cup **Parmesan cheese,** shredded, divided
2 cups **crabmeat** (if using king or snow, cut into bite-size pieces)
2 tablespoons fresh **parsley,** chopped

In a large sauté pan over medium heat; melt butter. Add garlic and sauté for 30 seconds. Add mushrooms and sauté until lightly browned. Add artichokes and wine, stirring for one minute. Add cream and ½ cup Parmesan; stir for another minute. Gently add crabmeat, then the reserved fettuccine and toss to coat.

Divide among pasta bowls and sprinkle with remaining Parmesan and chopped parsley.

CRAB IMPERIAL

Serves 4-6

½ cup **butter,** divided (melt 3 Tbls. for topping)
3 tablespoons all-purpose **flour**
2 cups **heavy cream**
1 cup Panko **bread crumbs,** divided
½ cup **red bell pepper,** diced
¼ cup **onion,** finely diced
4 tablespoons fresh **parsley,** minced and divided
2 tablespoons sherry **cooking wine**
2 tablespoons **lemon juice**
1 tablespoon **lime zest**
1½ teaspoons **Worcestershire sauce**
1 teaspoon **paprika,** divided
1 teaspoon ground **mustard**
½ teaspoon **Siracha hot sauce**
2 cups **crabmeat**
¾ teaspoon sea **salt**
¼ teaspoon ground black **pepper**
toasted **baguette slices,** for serving

Preheat your oven to 375˚F. In a large nonstick saucepan over medium heat, melt 5 tablespoons butter. Whisk in the flour. While whisking, slowly pour in the cream. Whisk until the mixture is thick and bubbly and coats the back of a spoon. Remove from heat and stir in ½ cup of the bread crumbs, the bell pepper, onion, 2 tablespoons parsley, wine, lemon juice, lemon zest, Worcestershire, ½ teaspoon paprika, mustard, hot sauce and crabmeat. Season with salt and pepper.

Divide mixture evenly among six 6-ounce oven-proof baking dishes (or four 1-cup); place on a rimmed baking sheet and set aside.

In a small bowl, mix remaining 3 tablespoons melted butter, ½ cup bread crumbs, ½ teaspoon paprika and ½ teaspoon parsley. Sprinkle evenly over each baking dish. Bake until lightly browned and bubbling in the center, about 20 minutes. Serve hot with the baguette toasts.

CRAB MAC & CHEESE

Serves 4

2½ cups **large elbow pasta**
6 tablespoons **butter**
½ cup **shallot,** finely diced
1 tablespoon **garlic,** minced
¼ cup all-purpose **flour**
2½ cups whole **milk**
⅛ teaspoon ground **nutmeg**
⅛ teaspoon dry **mustard**
½ teaspoons sea **salt**
¼ teaspoon ground black **pepper**
2 cups **sharp Cheddar cheese,** divided
½ cup **Fontina cheese,** shredded
½ cup **Parmesan cheese,** shredded and divided
2 cups **crabmeat** (if using king or snow, cut into bite-size pieces)
1 tablespoon fresh **parsley,** minced

Preheat your oven to 375˚F. In a large pot of salted boiling water, cook elbows according to package directions until al dente. Drain and return to pot.

Meanwhile, in a large skillet over medium heat, melt butter. Add shallots and garlic, sauté until soft. Add the flour and whisk until combined. Add the milk. Whisk until the mixture is thick and bubbly and coats the back of a spoon. Remove pan from heat.

Stir in the nutmeg, mustard, salt, pepper, 1½ cups Cheddar, Fontina and ¼ cup of the Parmesan. Gently add the crabmeat and the cooked elbows and stir until completely combined.

Sprinkle with remaining ½ cup Cheddar, ¼ cup Parmesan and the parsley and bake until bubbly, 20 minutes.

JUMBO LUMP CRAB POT PIE

Serves 4

1 sheet frozen **puff pastry, thawed**
4 tablespoons **butter**
1 cup **onion,** chopped
1 cup **carrot,** sliced ¼-inch thick
1 cup **celery,** sliced
1 cup button **mushrooms,** quartered
2 cups **red potatoes,** peeled and cubed
1½ teaspoons **Old Bay seasoning**
¼ teaspoon ground black **pepper**
½ cup all-purpose **flour**
⅓ cup sherry **cooking wine**
2 cups organic **chicken broth**
1 cup **half-and-half**
½ cup frozen **peas,** thawed
½ cup kernel **corn,** drained
2 cups **crabmeat** (if using king or snow, cut into bite-sized pieces)
1 egg, lightly beaten with 1 Tbls. milk

Preheat your oven to 350˚F. In a large saucepan, melt butter over medium heat. Add onions, carrots, celery, mushrooms and potatoes; stirring occasionally, until vegetables are just tender, 10 minutes. Stir in the Old Bay, pepper and flour. Add the wine, scraping bits from the bottom of the pan.

Gradually add broth and half-and-half, stirring until mixture is smooth. Cook and stir until thick and bubbly, about 10 to 15 minutes. Remove from heat and stir in the peas, corn and season with ½ tsp. salt and pepper. Gently add the crabmeat and transfer filling to a 2½-quart oven-proof baking dish.

On a lightly floured surface, roll the pastry to fit the baking dish. Arrange dough on filling and gently press it against the dish and crimp the edges. Make a small slit on top to allow the steam to escape. Transfer to a rimmed baking sheet lined with parchment paper. Brush dough with egg wash and bake pie until crust is golden, 30-40 minutes. Let stand 10 minutes before serving to set up.

KING CRAB LEGS WITH GARLIC-LEMON BUTTER

Serves 4

2 pounds **King Crab legs,** thawed
8 tablespoons (1 stick) **butter,** melted
5 cloves **garlic,** minced
1 tablespoon **lemon juice**
1 tablespoon fresh **parsley,** chopped
1 **lemon,** cut into wedges

Preheat your oven to 375˚F. Carefully using a sharp knife or a pair of scissors, cut the crab legs into halves to expose the meat. Arrange them evenly on a rimmed baking sheet. In a small saucepan, melt the butter. Stir in the garlic, lemon juice and parsley. Drizzle and brush the butter mixture on the crab legs and save some for dipping. Heat the crab legs in the oven for 5 minutes. Serve on a platter with the reserved garlic-lemon butter and lemon wedges.

PAN ROASTED KING CRAB

Serves 4

1 cup dry **white wine**
1 tablespoons **olive oil**
2 tablespoon **butter,** melted
1 **shallot,** chopped
1 teaspoon fresh **thyme,** chopped
½ teaspoon **red pepper flakes**
8 cloves **garlic,** minced
2 pounds **King Crab legs,** thawed
¼ cup fresh **parsley,** chopped

Preheat your oven to 350˚F. In a small saucepan, combine the wine, oil, butter, shallot, thyme, red pepper and garlic. Cook over medium-high heat for 3-4 minutes.

Place the whole, thawed legs in a large roasting pan, cover with the sauce and bake for 15 minutes, basting every few minutes with juices. Using tongs, remove the crab legs from the pan and place in bowls and pour roasting liquid over the top. Garnish with parsley and serve immediately.

SWEET TREATS

DATE BARS

Makes **16**

2 cups **Medjool dates,** pitted and finely chopped
½ cup **maple syrup**
1 cup **water**
1 teaspoon grated **lemon zest**
½ cup **butter,** softened
⅔ cup granulated **sugar**
1 cup all-purpose **flour**
1 cup **quick-cooking oats**
¼ teaspoon **baking soda**
¼ teaspoon sea **salt**

Preheat your oven to 375˚F. Spray an 11 x 7-inch oven-proof baking dish with nonstick cooking spray. In a saucepan over medium heat, combine the dates, maple syrup and water. Bring to a boil, cook 15 minutes or until most of the liquid is absorbed, stirring often. Stir in lemon zest, set aside to cool.

Meanwhile, using a hand mixer, cream the butter and sugar together on medium speed until well blended. Add the flour, oats, baking soda and salt until just combined. Press 2 cups of the flour mixture into the bottom of the baking dish. Spread the date mixture over the flour mixture. Sprinkle with remaining flour mixture. Bake for 20 minutes or until golden brown. Cool completely before serving.

LEMON BARS

Makes **16**

1½ cups **graham cracker crumbs**
6 tablespoons **butter,** melted
⅓ cup granulated **sugar**
1 (14-ounce) can **sweetened condensed milk**
5 **egg yolks**
½ cup **lemon juice**
2 tablespoons grated **lemon zest**
powdered sugar

Preheat your oven to 375˚F. Spray an 8-inch square pan with non-stick cooking spray and line with parchment paper.

Combine graham cracker crumbs, butter and sugar in a small bowl and stir until combined. Press the crumb mixture into the bottom of the prepared pan and press down firmly. Bake the crust for 7 minutes. Remove from the oven and let cool.

Lower your oven temperature to 350˚F. Whisk the sweetened condensed milk, egg yolks, lemon juice and zest together in a medium bowl. Pour over the cooled crust and bake for 25 minutes, until the filling is set. Let cool to room temperature.

Cut into squares and dust with powdered sugar.

FUDGE BROWNIES

Makes **16**

4 ounces **unsweetened chocolate baking squares**
¾ cup **butter**
1½ cups granulated **sugar**
½ cup firmly packed **brown sugar**
3 large **eggs**
1 cup all-purpose **flour**
1 teaspoon **vanilla** extract
⅛ teaspoon sea **salt**

Preheat your oven to 350˚F. Line bottom and sides of an 8 x 8-inch pan with parchment paper, allowing 2 to 3 inches to extend over sides. Lightly spray the parchment paper with nonstick cooking spray.

In a heat-proof bowl over a saucepan of simmering water, melt the chocolate and butter. Whisk in granulated and brown sugars. Add eggs one at a time, whisking just until blended after each addition. Whisk in flour, vanilla and salt. Pour mixture into prepared pan.

Bake for 35-40 minutes or until a wooden pick inserted in the center comes out with a few moist crumbs. Cool completely on a wire rack. Lift brownies from pan using parchment as handles. Gently remove parchment and cut brownies into 16 squares.

Mountain Bars

Makes **24**

½ cup **butter**
2 cups granulated **sugar**
½ cup baking **cocoa powder**
½ cup **milk**
1 teaspoon **vanilla extract**
½ cup crunchy **peanut butter**
3 cups **old-fashioned oats**

In a medium saucepan over medium heat, bring butter, sugar, cocoa and milk to a slow boil. Boil stirring constantly for exactly 3 minutes. Remove from heat, let cool for exactly 5 minutes. Gently add vanilla, peanut butter and oats. Drop by tablespoons onto a cookie sheet lined with parchment paper.

RHUBARB PIE

Serves 6
1 (9-inch) **unbaked pie crust**
1 pound (6 cups) fresh **rhubarb,** cut up
½ cup granulated **sugar**
1 tablespoon all-purpose **flour**

<u>Cream Cheese Layer</u>
4 ounces **cream cheese,** softened
½ cup granulated **sugar**
2 **eggs**

<u>Topping</u>
1 cup **sour cream**
2 tablespoons granulated **sugar**
1 teaspoon **vanilla** extract

Preheat your oven to 400°F. In a medium bowl, toss together the rhubarb, sugar and flour. Put in pie shell. Bake for 15 minutes. Remove from oven and set aside. Lower oven temperature to 350°F.

Cream Cheese Layer: Using a hand mixer, beat the cream cheese and sugar together on medium speed until well blended. Add eggs one at a time, until smooth. Pour over rhubarb layer in pie shell and bake for 30 minutes.

Topping: In a small bowl, blend together the sour cream, sugar and vanilla. Spread on hot pie. Cool completely before cutting.

INDEX OF RECIPES

NIBBLES

Brie & Crab Dip   18
Jumbo Lump Crab Cocktail   19
Crab Stuffed Mushrooms   20,21
Crab Rangoon   22
Crab Sauté   23
Soft Spring Rolls with Crab   24,25
Crab Cakes   26
Crostini with Avocado & Crab   27
Crab Croquettes   28,29
Crab Louie Wonton Cups   30
Mini Crab Quiches   31
Crab Salad on Corn Blini   32

BRUNCH & LUNCH

Crab Strata   36
Frittata with Crab & Chorizo   37
Crab Eggs Benedict   38,39
Rustic Crab Quiche   40
Crab Strudel   41
Crab Delight   42
Grilled Crab Reuben   43
Caramelized Garlic & Crab Tart   44
Crab Louie Sandwich   45
Margarita Crab Pizza   46,47
Crab BLT Sandwich   48
Crab Cake Po' Boy   49

SOUPS & SALADS

Potato-Fennel Crab Soup   52
Avocado-Crab & Tomato Towers   53
Spicy Crab Veggie Soup   54,55
Crab Curry Soup   56

Crab Corn Chowder	57
Homemade Crab Salsa	58,59
Crab Louie	60
Crab-Avocado & Mango Quinoa Bowl	61
Crab Caesar Salad	62
Avocado Crab Boats	63

MAIN DISHES

Dungeness Crab Legs with Four Sauces	66,67
Crab Tacos	68,69
Creamy Crabmeat Fettuccine	70
Crab Imperial	71
Crab Mac & Cheese	72,73
Jumbo Lump Crab Pot Pie	74
King Crab Legs with Garlic - Lemon Butter	75
Pan Roasted King Crab	75

SWEET TREATS

Date Bars	78
Lemon Bars	79
Fudge Brownies	80,81
Mountain Bars	82
Rhubarb Pie	83

We hope you enjoy this book as much as we enjoyed creating it and we truly hope you put it to good use. It would make us happy to have this cookbook become your trusty kitchen companion. Please wrinkle the pages, dust it with crumbs and use it often.

Best Fishes!
Ole & LaDonna Rose

OTHER COOKBOOKS BY
LaDonna Gundersen
Available at ladonnarose.com
facebook.com/ladonnarosecooks
instagram.com/ladonnarosecooks

#boat2table

The End

NOTES